The right image

Dave Boyle
Wendy Pitt

CAMBRIDGE
UNIVERSITY PRESS

Published by the Press Syndicate of the University of Cambridge
The Pitt Building, Trumpington Street, Cambridge CB2 1RP
40 West 20th Street, New York, NY 10011–4211, USA
10 Stamford Road, Oakleigh, Victoria 3166, Australia

In association with Staffordshire County Council

© Cambridge University Press 1992

First published 1992

Printed in Great Britain by Scotprint Limited, Musselburgh

Designed and Produced by Gecko Limited, Bicester, Oxon.

A catalogue record of this book is available from the British Library.

ISBN 0 521 40622 6

PICTURE ACKNOWLEDGEMENTS

Christopher Coggins 12, 27, 30.
Sally and Richard Greenhill 8.
Robert Harding Picture Library 11bl.
Judy Harrison 24, 25t, 25b, 26tr, 26b.
Images 11tr.
Rob Judges 9.
Last Resort 17tr.
Photofusion 16bl.
David Richardson 25c, 26c.
Picturesport Associates 11tl, 11tc, 11bl, 11br.
Frank Spooner Pictures 16tr, 17tl.
Zefa Ltd. 16br, 17b.

Picture Research by Linda Proud

NOTICE TO TEACHERS

The contents of this book are in the copyright of
Cambridge University Press. Unauthorised
copying of any of the pages is not only illegal but
also goes against the interests of the authors.

For authorised copying please check that your
school has a licence (through the Local Education
Authority) from the Copyright Licensing Agency
which enables you to copy small parts of the text
in limited numbers.

Contents

Clothes people wear   4

Changing Images   16

Clothes *people wear*

Talking together

What clothes do people wear during the course of a day?
How are these clothes chosen?
Where can you buy clothes?
Where are they stored until wanted?
When are special clothes worn?
Which clothes are needed to protect against:
- water
- sun
- fire
- cold
- wind

What materials are clothes made from?
How are clothes kept clean?

5

A need

You have been asked to design a new range of winter clothing. You need to find out what people like and dislike about winter clothes.

Developing your design

Planning your ideas

What colours do people enjoy wearing?
What materials do they like their clothes to be made from?
What materials are most suitable for winter clothes?
What colours and materials do people dislike?
How much do they want to pay for their clothes?

• D A T A   F I L E •

Research:
data collection and display

Consumer research

One of the things you may have to carry out as part of your investigation is consumer research.

You may need to design a questionnaire to help you to collect this information.

How would this information be useful if you were going to make some new clothes to sell?

ONLY **ONE** PERSON LIKED THIS FABRIC!

NINE PEOPLE LIKE THIS COLOUR

YUK!

I LIKE THE RED!

BLUE HAS COME OUT THE MOST POPULAR COLOUR FOR COATS

Testing materials

You will need to find out whether the materials you are going to suggest for a new range of clothing are suitable or not. To help you to choose the most suitable materials you will need to carry out some tests.

What do you want to find out about the materials you are going to use?
What tests do you need to carry out?

• DATA FILE •
Fair testing

9

A need

When the school sports kit is taken out of the store room you find that some mice have made a nest in the kit. To make their nest they have nibbled holes in it. Time for a new kit for the school team!

Developing your design

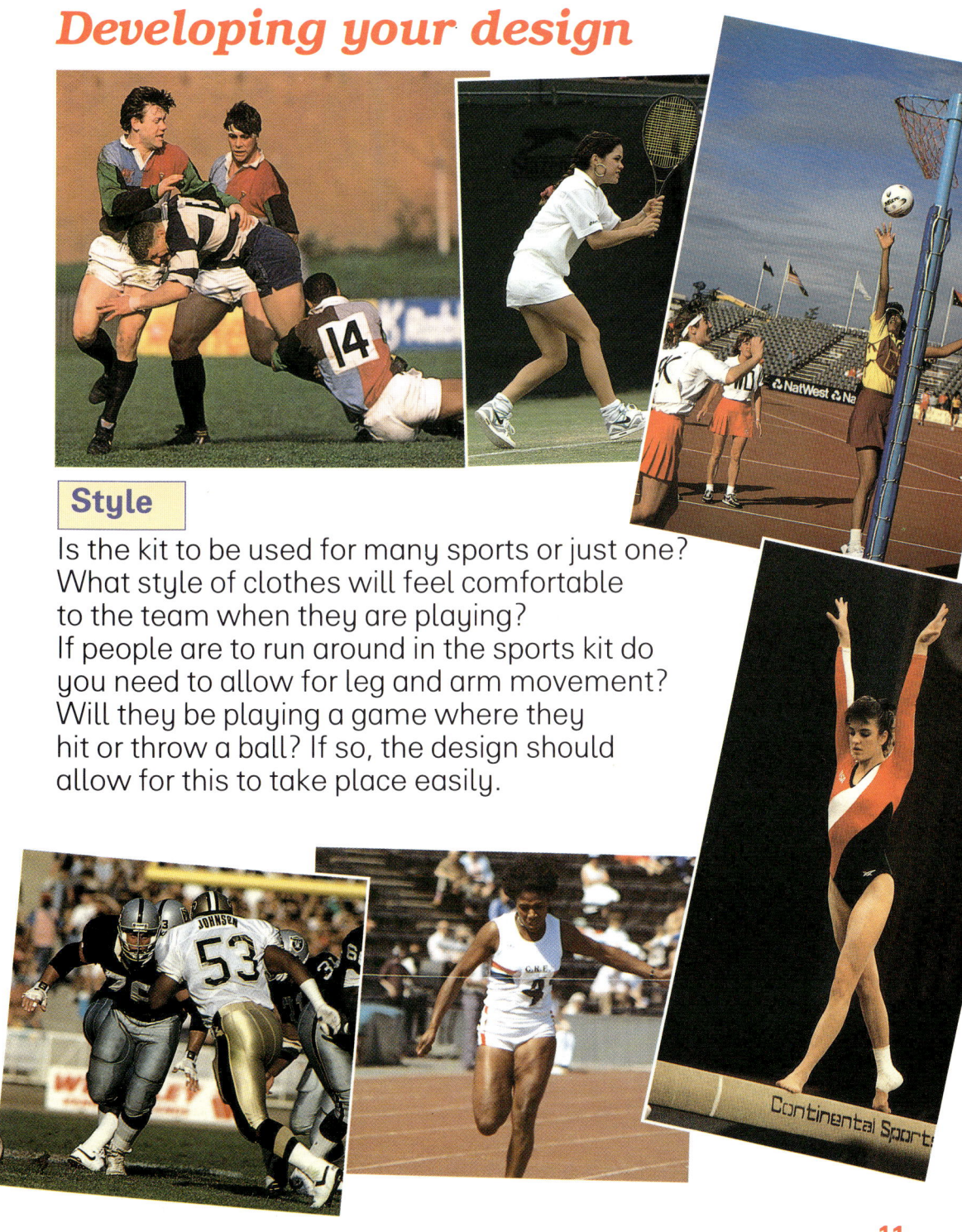

Style

Is the kit to be used for many sports or just one? What style of clothes will feel comfortable to the team when they are playing? If people are to run around in the sports kit do you need to allow for leg and arm movement? Will they be playing a game where they hit or throw a ball? If so, the design should allow for this to take place easily.

Colour

What colours could be used for the kit?

Perhaps you have school colours that could be used in different ways. There might be a need for home and away kits which could be different colours.

Materials

Which materials could be used to make the kit?

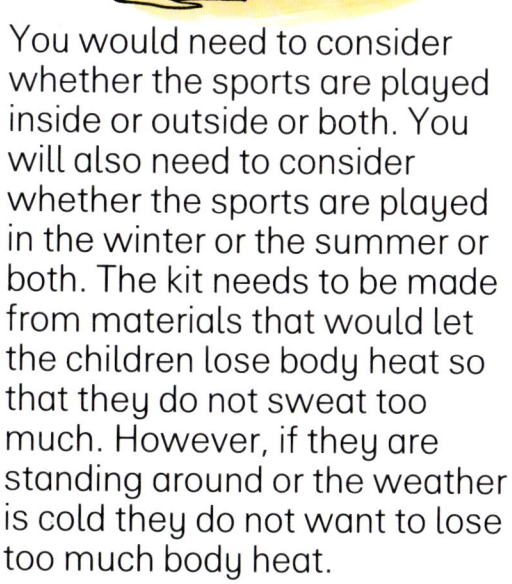

You would need to consider whether the sports are played inside or outside or both. You will also need to consider whether the sports are played in the winter or the summer or both. The kit needs to be made from materials that would let the children lose body heat so that they do not sweat too much. However, if they are standing around or the weather is cold they do not want to lose too much body heat.

• D A T A   F I L E •

Fabrics:
joining
sewing
adding something extra
working with
making
making and using templates
and patterns
dyeing
using fabric crayons,
pens and paint

13

Choosing a design

How will the best design be chosen?
There could be a display of all the designs
and materials.
Children could see all the different
suggestions and vote for the one they
prefer. The chosen design could then be
used for the new kit.

• D A T A   F I L E •
**Presentation
Advertising methods**

More ideas

When the team travel to the away matches they sometimes need to have a tracksuit to keep them warm.
Design a suitable tracksuit that would match the team kit.

After some matches the players can take a shower.
Design a bag that would be suitable for carrying the things they would need for a shower.

The team kit will need to be stored somewhere the mice will not be able to get to it.
Can you design and make something suitable in which to store the kit?

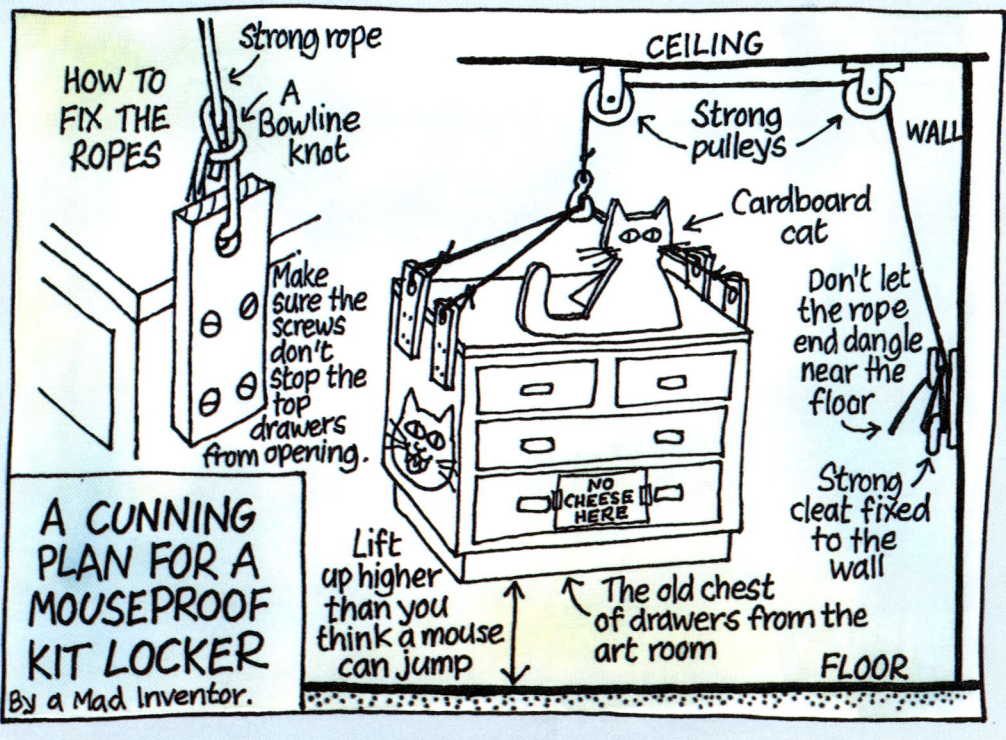

A CUNNING PLAN FOR A MOUSEPROOF KIT LOCKER
By a Mad Inventor.

HOW TO FIX THE ROPES
Strong rope
A Bowline knot
Make sure the screws don't stop the top drawers from opening.

CEILING
Strong pulleys
WALL
Cardboard cat
Don't let the rope end dangle near the floor
Strong cleat fixed to the wall

Lift up higher than you think a mouse can jump
NO CHEESE HERE
The old chest of drawers from the art room
FLOOR

15

Changing Images

Talking together

Can you sort the clothes into different groups?
Can the different fabrics be sorted?
What materials are clothes made from?
How are these various materials manufactured?

Are any clothing materials treated to make them:
- flameproof
- dirt proof
- scuff proof
- waterproof
- wind proof

How are they treated?

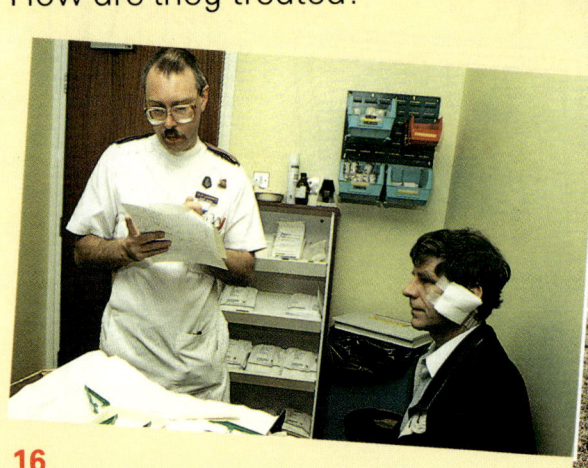

17

How are the patterns put onto fabrics?
What kinds of patterns are fashionable now?
What colours are in fashion?
How could you start a fashion trend?

Is fabric used for anything other than clothes?

A need

The school computer covers need replacing. You need to make new covers that are attractive. They could have your school logo and name prominently displayed on them.

Developing your design

Dyeing

Cold water dyes can be used to change the colour of fabric. The dyes can be mixed with cold water. This solution can be used to change the colour of the fabric. The fabric will need to be tested first to find out whether it will take the dye. How can you test the fabric?

Follow maker's instructions when mixing and using the dye.

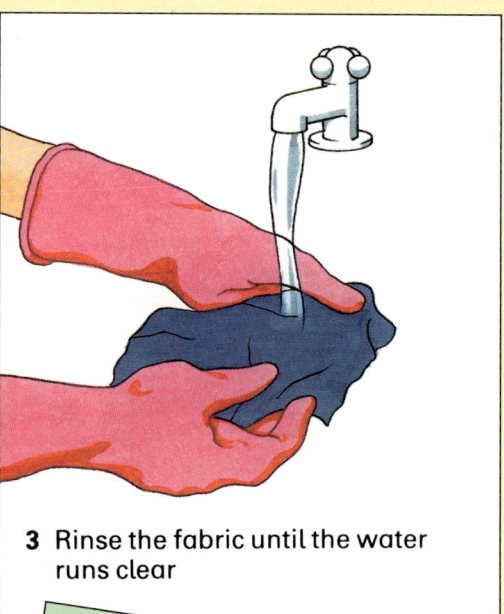

2 Put the fabric into the dye solution. Let it soak for the recommended time.

Testing a sample

1 Wash the fabric and leave it wet.

3 Rinse the fabric until the water runs clear

• D A T A   F I L E •
Preparing myself
Preparing your work area:
painting and printing
Fabrics:
dyeing

20

Tie and dye

Tie and dye is often used to make patterns on fabric. You can tie patterns into the fabric. You can also tie solid objects in the fabric to produce a pattern.

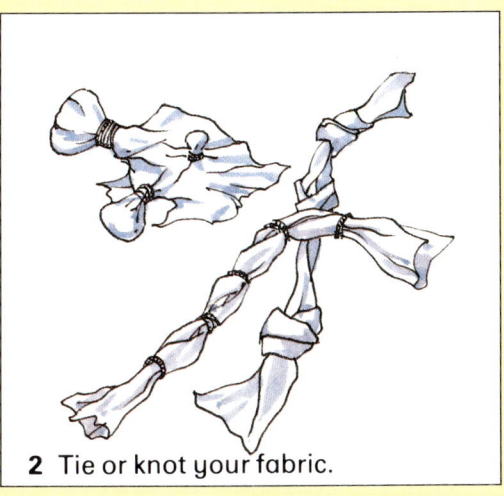

1 Wash your fabric and leave it wet.

2 Tie or knot your fabric.

3 Soak it in the dye solution.

4 Rinse the fabric until the water runs clear.

Using fabric crayons

Fabric crayons can be used to decorate fabric. Your teacher can iron the pattern onto the fabric so that the colours do not wash out.
As the pattern comes out back to front, remember to draw everything back to front.

Tape the fabric flat on a board.

You can draw straight onto the fabric with some crayons and paints.

Printing onto fabric

You can print onto fabric by using vegetables such as potatoes. You can try many ideas and decide which of the patterns you prefer before you print onto the fabric.

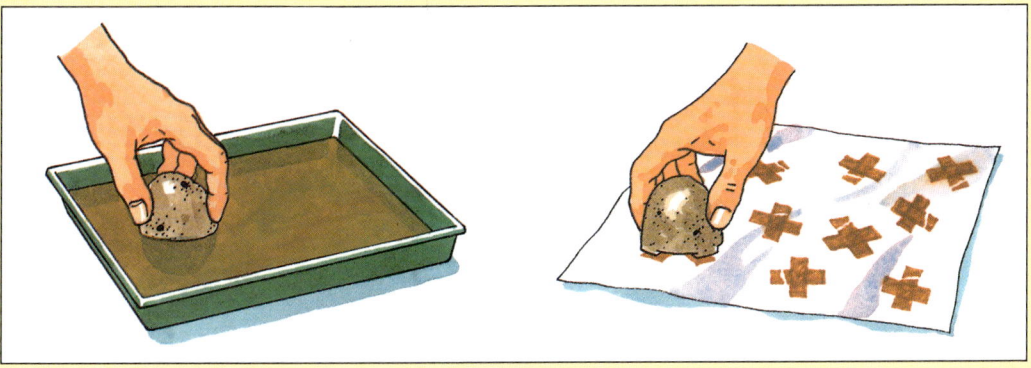

Ask your teacher before using craft knives.

• DATA FILE •
Preparing myself
Preparing your work area:
painting and printing
Fabrics:
using fabric crayons, pens and paint
Printing:
using potatoes
using blocks and rollers

A need

You have been asked to make some models for an exhibition to show the different costumes needed for a school play. This will help people decide what are the most suitable costumes for the production.

> Divali celebrations often include the story of Prince Rama and Princess Sita. Sita was captured by a demon king. Eventually, with help from the monkey army and other animals, Rama found and rescued Sita.

Preparing for a Divali play

Developing your design

Planning your ideas

What is the play about? How many characters are there in the play? Who are they?
Which costumes do you want to make for your exhibition?

Scenes from Divali plays.

25

Drawing your ideas

People who design clothing need to make many drawings of their ideas. The drawings can be looked at and a choice made. Once a choice is made the costumes can be made in the designer's style and materials.

• D A T A   F I L E •

Graphics:
design sheet

Using models

You could make models from plasticine or playdough which could be dressed in a variety of ways to show the costume ideas. These models may be dressed in small examples of the costumes designed for the production.

• DATA FILE •
Doughlike materials
Fabrics:
joining
sewing
adding something extra
working with
making and using templates and patterns

Making a template

You could make a template of a figure and then dress it in the suggested costumes for the production.

28

Displaying your models

Do you need to make a background so that people can see how effective the costumes are?
How big is this exhibition to be?
Will the models stand up on their own or do you need to make them more stable?
You may need to make a stand for your models to rest on.

• DATA FILE •
Card and paper:
cutting
joining
Structures:
stability

Lighting your exhibit

To give some special effects, the exhibit can be lit using simple circuits.

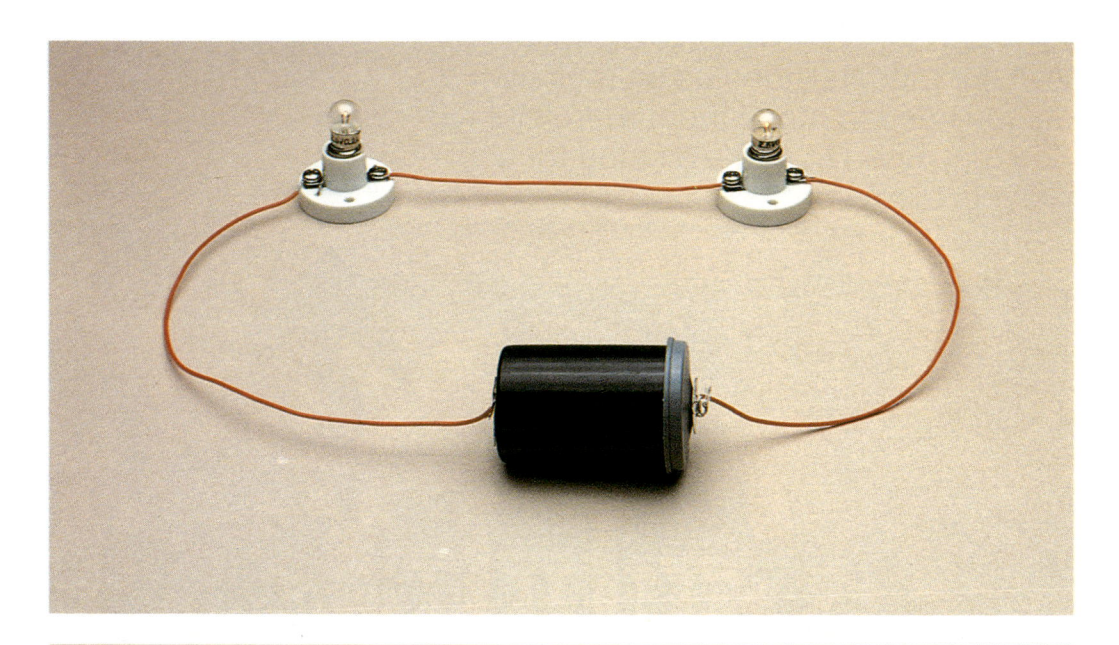

• DATA FILE •
Electricity:
simple circuits 1
simple circuits 2

You could design a circuit so that the lights can be turned on and off to give different effects.

• D A T A F I L E •

Electricity:
switches 1
switches 2

31

More ideas

The local playgroup have asked your class to design some protective aprons for the toddlers when they are painting.

You would like to personalise your games bag. This would stop it getting lost in the cloakroom. You need to design and print a special logo for it.

As part of your history project your group would like to mount a clothing exhibition. The theme of the exhibition is 'Fashion in the '60s and 70s'. This exhibition would be used on an open evening when the local community have been invited to come to school and to see your history project.